KIDS SURE RITE FUNNY!

Kids Sure Rite Funny!

A Child's
Garden of Misinformation

LOVINGLY HARVESTED BY

ART LINKLETTER

Illustrated by Whitney Darrow, Jr.

PUBLISHED BY BERNARD GEIS ASSOCIATES
DISTRIBUTED BY RANDOM HOUSE

This book is dedicated to the School Kids of America. In their running leaps at the high-jump bar of knowledge, they sometimes come a cropper—and some of their best "croppers" are included in this book—but thank goodness they always dust themselves off, set the bar a notch higher, and try, try again!

—ART LINKLETTER

Contents

Foreword

D ID YOU KNOW that a bunkhouse is where cowboys go to tell how brave they are, and other such bunk? Or that the ash around volcanoes was once hot java? That "double jeopardy" means being arrested by more than one jeopardy sheriff? Or that a baby born today can expect to have a longer gevity than his parents?

Somewhere in America are some earnest little scholars who are convinced that all these lopsided and off-center bits of knowledge are literally true. In fact, these youngsters wrote every one of them as answers on examination papers at school—much to the delight of their teachers.

I've been on a laughing jag ever since I started in as your editor of this book, which is a silly sampler of hundreds of the funniest classroom boners, bloopers and howlers ever written. Most of this joyful crop of educational absurdities was lovingly harvested by a Missouri schoolteacher, Harold Dunn. When I first sat down to read Mr. Dunn's manuscript, I thought he'd done a marvelous job. I was so carried away that I fattened the manuscript with several dozen of my own classroom favorites that teachers, listeners to my "House Party" show, and readers have been sending me over the years.

It isn't easy to define a boner, any more than a comedian can explain exactly why a certain gag gets big laughs, but let's try:

Boners are far more than a childish slip of the pen on examination day. They are never *intended* to be funny—they just turn out that way.

A kid in school is like a chemist in a laboratory. He's constantly testing and experimenting, combining what he knows with other things that *seem* to make sense. Ordinarily the mixture is a success—but sometimes the result is a boner that blows up and rocks the lab with laughter.

Here's what I consider a perfect example of a child's mind at work, as he attempts to combine what teacher says with what he is beginning to sense of the vast, confusing world around him:

"Once there was this Nathan Hale who was a spy. But not a onrinary spy. He was a good one. Even when cought he knew what was right, so he died rather happily ever after."

Obviously the young writer of this little essay had

been taught that Nathan Hale had died gloriously and heroically. But he didn't quite understand what this meant, so he came up with that unique expression about dying happily ever after. I suspect that afterward the boy thought it over, sensed that people don't *really* die happily ever after, and hedged a little by saying that Hale died "rather" happily. No adult could possibly write such a thing, because only the eager, half-tutored mind of a child could conceive of it.

Here's another highly imaginative idea that might never occur to a grownup:

"Eating onions gives some protection from the breathing of others eating onions. But the only sure way is for mankind to get together and agree to destroy all his stockpile of eatable onions."

I wonder how the United Nations would feel about an onion disarmament program. . . . Personally, I'm all for keeping our onion stockpile as a strong deterrent. In fact, maybe we'd be wise to set up a testing program immediately on the most breathtaking weapon of all—garlic!

Before I put down my editor's pencil, I'd like to say one last and heartfelt word about that eternal and unchanging creature, the child. Most parents, I've found, are fairly sophisticated about the basic theories of child psychology. They're far different in their attitudes as compared with their own grandparents, who were shocked when Sigmund Freud first described the infant as an egomaniacal tyrant, full of rages, hungers and dark impulses. Today we've come to accept the idea that from earliest childhood, we are bundles of frustrations and destructive urges, all held down none too securely under the lids of our ids.

But what can we say of the sweet, trusting innocence of childhood . . . its shy charm . . . its bright, quicksilver beauty . . . the dreaming wonder in a child's eyes? These are the great themes of the wisest of all knowers of the human heart, our poets. Only a Carl Sandburg can sing of the laughter of children who tumble barefooted and bareheaded in the summer grass. Only a Shelley can remind us what it's like to be a child. . . . "It is to have a spirit yet streaming from the waters of baptism; it is to believe in love, to believe in loveliness, to believe in belief; it is to be so little that the elves can reach to whisper in your ear; it is to turn pumpkins into coaches, and mice into horses, lowness into loftiness, and nothing into everything, for each child has its fairy godmother in its soul."

It is in this spirit that we should journey through these pages . . . and I can think of no better guide to set our feet upon the path than one of my favorite poets, William Blake, who was so very like a child at heart himself. It was Blake who sang of the merry innocence of the young with these lines:

Piping down the valleys wild,
Piping songs of pleasant glee,
On a cloud I saw a child.

So let's be off on our skylark of laughs with the
school kids, who are eager to tell you all about such
famous people as Robinson Caruso, the opera singer
who was shipwrecked, and that great French fashion
designer, Plaster of Paris. You'll also learn such fascinating things as what turtles think about their
gooey beds, why grasshoppers are so jumpy, why
the Egyptians all wanted to be mommies, and how
to undress a stranger properly. You're in for fun every
step of the way, because—*Kids Sure Rite Funny!*

KIDS SURE RITE FUNNY!

CHAPTER 1

The Best They Is in English

IF IT hadn't been for the need to pursue groceries as well as knowledge back in my college days, I might today be parading across some campus quadrangle in cap and gown as Professor Arthur Gordon Linkletter, Doctor of Literature. English was always my favorite subject, and the thought of becoming a professor was tremendously appealing. After all, it offered the daily challenge of ideas in the classroom . . . the respect of the community . . . and something called "tenure," which is an educator's delicate way of describing a steady job. But before this dream of a well-rounded education could come true, I had to find a way of providing a few well-rounded meals. I found I could earn the money I needed after classes by making announcements on a local radio station. What began that way as a temporary sidetracking of my academic career became the career itself, and my visions of an ivy-clad Linkletter gradually faded away. My old love for our language is still there, however, and I wince whenever some sharp-eared listener fires a postcard at me, catching me up in some technical slip I've made in English on the air.

If college graduates still lose their way occasionally in the mazes of English grammar, you can imagine how bewildered our school kids can be. Learning to write compositions is almost as hard as learning to talk all over again. As one pupil put it, "There is a difference between being able to talk orally and writenly."

Let's examine a few samples of "talking writenly," starting with a free-swinging little sermon on that awful word "got":

"There is no use even ever saying Got. Like some say, we have Got a pencil. It would be more right to say, we have a pencil. I for one know never to say G— that word anymore."

If you're ever mixed up on the use of "can" and "may," here's a tip from a little boy who understands the difference quite well:

"Can means we can do anything we want to and nobody is going to stop us, and may means maybe we better ask anyway."

The English may be slightly fractured, but the idea comes through in one piece in this lesson on sentences: "When you are I, he, she, or they, you are in the subjective and are doing things. But when you are me, him, her, or them, you are in the objective and they are doing it back to you."

If you're at all hazy about that old English buga-boo, the double negative, hang on. Here are some thoughts that will leave you only slightly worse off than before:

"Anyone that says not and no in the same sentence is really saying yes. And that goes for n't too."

"If you are remarking 'I don't want to nohow' you are actually remarking 'I do.' This can lead to a mis-understanding."

Punctuation is another puzzler, but few kids are quite as confused as the little boy who defined it this way:

"Good punctuation means not to be late."

Another boy, who does his outside reading in comic books, wrote this:

"Sometimes punctuation marks all speak of the same thing, like #%*! and & are all saying darn you."

Let's leaf through a few more copybooks for thoughts on the art of "talking writenly":

Allthough I am rather weak in biology, I am the best they is in English class.

When a person is in too much of a hurry to say pound, he can say lb.

If I should say period, what I mean would depend on if I said it in English or history.

Some co-pupils I have known never knew when to use a question mark?

Compounds can be studied in either chemistry or sentences.

In order to write a compound sentence, a person must have at least one coma.

People have sex while nouns have genders.

Don't use commas, that aren't necessary.

"Don't" is a contraption.

Italics are what the Italians write in.

You put a question mark at the end of a sentence to
  show that your voice should go up?

Will I pass English this year and why not?

"At the bedside," is a propositional phrase.

An adverb is an added verb for the purpose of who
  knows why?

(*Give the antonym of upright.*)
  Downright.

(*What is the antonym of woe?*)
  Geddyup.

In saying do not in a qwick way, you may say don't.
  Of course it takes some time to learn when to say
  it, so it is about six of one and one for all.

Here is some English to be known. Whom instead of who. Never ai'nt. Diagraming also.

I am rather unclear about sing sang and sung. If I do it right now I know it is that I sing. But if I did it say yesterday I am not clear what I did.

Poultry has a singular, known as chicken.

Radium's plural is radius.

(*Give the antonym of shiftless.*)
    Shifty.

We should always say deer when we mean two or
more deers.

We must remember that a p-h is often used in place
of an f. For some people go through life entirely
never learning how to spell correctly such words
as phoebia.

One of the important things to decide in studying for
an English test is whether to figure out the questions to be asked or to study for answers and not
be sure of the questions.

Most words are easy for me to spell once I get the
letters right.

* is an asterick. It is a reminder to go look some
place else if you want to know the whole truth.

To write a story in the first person means to write
it like Adam would.

Most longer words can be abrevated.

The plural of monument is biument. But they are so
costy we don't need to learn the word for so
many.

When we have finished resting we have *lain*. No one
has ever *laid* (at least in this class).

(*Use the word "assume" in a sentence.*)
I would just assume be grown as like I am.

Upon hearing the phrase "spinning a yarn" we must
stop and think. Think weather it is about sewing
or story telling.

CHAPTER 2

How To Undress a Stranger

ONE OF my favorite characters in literature has always been Mrs. Malaprop, that hilarious lady in Sheridan's immortal play of the 18th century, *The Rivals*. Mrs. Malaprop made so many blunders in the use of words that we now use her name to describe the type of mistakes she made with the language.

Some of the funniest malaprops ever written, however, did not come from the pen of Sheridan and were quite unintentional. They were scrawled out on copybook paper by our school kids, like this little pointer on etiquette:

"I try to always be formal but polite when undressing a stranger."

Kids are natural malaproppers, because so many words sound alike to them but have meanings that are miles apart. At least half the battle of learning what a word *means,* after all, is making sure what it *doesn't* mean.

Imagine how teacher must have laughed when she ran across such genuine malaprops as these:

"My sister is a mistress at Shorty's Cafe."

"I will have my bookie report tomorrow."

"My brother is suffering from indolent fever."

"Yes, Thanksgiving is truly a time of happiness for every child, adult and adultress."

"Mother wants my sister to take biology next year but she has a mind of her own. She's at that obstetric age."

I've had skeptics corner me at parties and insist that the kids I interview on my "House Party" show just couldn't be that funny, day after day, without some backstage gagwriting by grownups. That's non-sense—and I'll tell you why. Kids are fresh, original and offbeat in their thinking because it's the only way they *can* be. They're not like us lazy-minded adults, who can reach into our lifetime stockpile of common expressions for a ready-made way of saying what we wish. The child has no stockpile, so he's forced to think through his ideas for himself, and then *make up* an expression that seems to fit.

Let's look at the contrast between the conventional grownup and a little boy as both react to one of life's lesser tragedies, the inevitable appearance of Mondays after those carefree and enjoyable Saturdays and Sundays. The grownup already has a pat expression at hand in the old stockpile to tell how he feels . . . "Blue Monday." But a little boy who just couldn't believe there could be so many Mondays had to think it through, and then checked the facts for himself before he made this solemn report to his classmates:

"Looking at a calendar will prove there are not actually any more Mondays than Saturdays."

Sometimes a child is caught in the cross fire between the high ideals of the classroom and the realities of everyday behavior. One boy who bravely reached for the heights of honesty came crashing down with this confession:

"Because of George Washington, I once told the truth even though I thought I might get into trouble. I was right."

Another young seeker of truth proclaimed, "It is more important to be honest than rich and famous and happy." Then the idea began melting away on him like a popsicle, as he added, "Or at least any one of these by itself. In most cases."

Imagine how a certain instructor felt when a pupil wrote this comment at the end of a semester:

"This course in philosophy was a great help to me, personally. Although I used to be rather confused and lack confidence in my thinking, I am now confident to know that we are all rather confused."

Confusion seems to be taking over completely as we wander onward now through this child's garden of nonsense and examine some of the choicer confessions of our bewildered young scholars:

I am unsure about Daylight Savings Time. Maybe you can explain it to me. I can't.

I plan to get a brod education.

One of the unusualities about my family is that my cousin also happens to be the son of my father's sister.

Besides my mother and father, I have a fellow-sister and three bothers.

Once my gang bilt a club house but there was onaly room for 1 at a time.

My sister is sex and a half.

Mother says use plenty of eggs in the milk to make a good omen.

Some good table manners are not to put your fingers in the butter and stop standing on that chair.

The Holloween party I went to last year wasn't too much. I only screamed twise.

It is often only a matter of fate as to whether a person is a genius or not. I, for example, (knowing what I do) would be one had I only been born 1000 years ago.

Last Halloween's movie was about a vampire that bit other peoples necks and just went out and bit somebody else when he was hungray again. I got so tickled.

I have on occasion dranken coffee. I like it black, mixed half and half with cream.

The ice cream and cookies really hit my spot after being in the sun all that while.

We are not to run in class even when teacher don't see us because even if teacher don't see us Jesus can and he might tell the principal.

Polite means to say thank you when you don't really want to.

Ties are a great source of comfort when taken off.

We soon discovered our new used car had defected brakes.

Though I am now a child, I will one day be a man or a woman.

I have had many good ideas for inventions in the past, but couldn't think how to use them.

If I get to feeling funny about the length of my dresses, I just let the hims out.

When we first moved in, our house was quite rambled by lack of upkeep.

Santa's reindeer get around so fast because they have athletes feet.

When I see a sad television, I try to keep my composure, but I often get completely decomposed.

I particularly enjoy candid apples.

You can strike a happy medium by doing it this way.
First pay the fortune teller but then hit her right
after.

I plan to be married one day. Longer than one day
really. It is just that this is how it is usually said.

From two to two:30 last year we of our class drew. Pictures. No guns.

When I can go up on a hill and look down on our city it has a very sooting influence on me.

According to some peoples beliefs, there is something that is half way between heaven and hell. It's called pubertory.

Women like to sew in circles, where they knit, talk and do their needling.

I have been told thrashing machines are not really used on children.

I have been brought up never to break my bread or roll in my soup.

By the time we finally arrived at my uncle's house, I was ready to eat anything. Needless to say I was eager to see my new baby cousin.

I have resolved this year not to fight my sister unless she fights me first or makes me mad or I feel like it.

CHAPTER 3

Turtles Have Gooey Beds

OLD MAN NOAH managed to crowd many a strange creature aboard his Ark, but few of his seagoing menagerie are half so fascinating as the curious animals and insects that inhabit the fantasy world of our school kids. Let's go for a nature walk in these next few pages, and learn the answers to some of nature's most intriguing secrets . . . why grasshoppers are so jumpy . . . all about the quaint habits of that queer-type bird, the oscridge . . . and what turtles really think of their gooey beds.

Much of the fun in talking to kids comes from the startling way they can put a backspin on their answers, saying something that's ridiculous and sensible at the same time. One young nature lover, asked how he would mount a butterfly, replied with devastating logic:

28

"About like a horse if you can get one big enough."

Butterflies the size of the winged Pegasus must surely exist some place, the boy reasons, because you certainly couldn't mount one of those little ones that flit from flower to flower.

Kids are so full of questions that they can't possibly wait for someone to tell them all the answers. That's why they plunge recklessly ahead on their own, like so:

"We used to deepend on silkworms excluesively until we noticed rayonworms and nylonworms."

"When the frogs are in the water as tadpoles, they get in a bad habit of eating their own tails. Only on land is a frog safe from eating hisself up before it is too late."

"When whales spout, they do because they enjoy smoking water."

Sometimes an earnest young mind comes up with an entirely new theory, as this boy did:

"The skin from many kinds of animals is used to make clothes. I think we should watch these animals closer. For if we see them scraching, we should know it will scrach us two."

Here's another provocative bit of logical advice that a little girl had for snakes. She said, "When snakes eat too much or too fast, there skin pops off. They should take time to think about it."

It may surprise you to see how serious a child can be when he is thinking about his own origin and place here on earth. He learns soon enough that human beings are masters of the earth, and that other animals are under man's dominion. He sees the animals in the zoo, in the barnyard, and the pets at home all dependent upon the will of man. After thinking about this, here is what one young man wrote to account for it:

"While other animals were just playing around and having a good time, man was hard at work thinking how to evolve."

Of all the questions that a child has on his mind, he is fascinated most by the ones that begin with "why." As any weary mother knows, the little ones under her feet are always saying why this and why that. With such a large supply of "whys" and a very small supply of "becauses," it's no wonder that a child would come up with a merry-go-round kind of essay like this:

"A grasshopper is nervous and jumpy because he cannot sleep. He cannot sleep because he has no eyelids. He has no eyelids because he is too nervous and jumpy to sleep."

And so on and on.

There are times when even the truth sounds unbelievable to a child's ear. Tell a little boy that fish live in schools, and he automatically pictures a classroom, complete with teacher. So you can hardly blame the boy who wrote this:

"When fish get together they are in schools. Yes, they are. I can show where it says."

And another skeptic wrote, "Although a whale has now been discovered to be a mammal, there are still some fishy things about it."

Here are more novel nature notes:

Perching birds enjoy sitting on that kind of fish.

The home for a pet turtle should have two inches of dirt in it with three inches of water. Don't worry because he likes gooey beds.

Turtles eat worms, lettuce and turtle food that they
　　buy in any pet shop.

Box turtles are land turtles. They make good pests.

Hamsters carry their meals in their pockets and their
　　pockets in their cheeks.

Watch out if you see a rouge elephant!

One good way I figured out to tell between the buf-
　　falo and bison is one of them is bigger than the
　　other when I can think which it is.

The lesser anteater is called the tamandua. We can
　　only guess what is called the greater one.

Mad dogs must be shot as we have no way of telling
who they are mad at and might bite.

Sardines are vanishing rapidly off the coast of California, so they are something we should stop
talking about being packed as tight as.

(*Give the names of two bears that inhabit the Far
North.*)
They have polar bears and brown Kodak bears
up there, but I don't know any of their names.

Wild bores are the worst kind of pigs.

The zebra looks funny to us because it is stripped.

We know something strange about birds. Altho they have no teeth they like to eat gravel.

The flycatcher uses snake skins in its nest. Oh. After the snakes are through with them.

An octopus gets its name from knowing how to have eight baby octopusses at once.

I also read that pet rabitts are soft and gentle and
    quiet. The book did not menshun quiet what.

Pet racoons will wash their food if you give them a
    pain.

The maltese cat is that because it likes malts.

Cream, fish and liver are all good cat foods. Their most tasty would probly be creamed fish liver.

Some dogs are toy dogs but not really.

A silk worm has not one but tee-double U-oh! holes in his head. But instead of siting and sulking he uses them to make silk.

Nowaday horses are a vanishing race.

Beavers are wonderful at dammi I should say making water holes with branches.

The Scorpion was the pioneer of all the land animals. I think history will decide he is just as important as Columbus.

All tigers have stripped skins.

The Salamand is the wisest of all the river creatures. I have heard stories about the wisdom of a Salamand that are almost unbelievable.

The clam has no other bones except on its outsides.

Dogs age much quicker than people. In less than two months they are a year old.

It is the male that says "Katy did!" He has to hang upside down and rub his wings together but it's worth it to him I guess.

Back when animals first began having babies we had to have a name for them. So we called them litters. Bugs too. Litters for riding were later type litters.

Painted turtles got their names by living in the painted desert.

Because of their extra good hearing, dogs often helped heard sheep.

Owls pray mostly on rodents.

Now that the dinosaurs are safely dead, we can call them clumsy and stupid.

While most birds sit on eggs to hatch, the nuthatch has other ideas.

Otters have more fun than most anybody else.

Viscious dogs should be shut up. Or at leash on a least when walking.

A sheep-dog is what you get from mixing sheeps and dogs.

The greyhound's long legs and skinny body makes, of all dogs, him the most rabid.

Some silly super-stitious people still think it is as much bad luck to walk under a ladder as to see a black cat.

While cod and whiting are certainly popular with
many people, others would just as soon eat
mackinaw.

Here is a queer-type bird. A oscridge that does not
fly but runs like a horse. Except he uses two legs
which makes him a queer-type horse, too.

The honeycomb is used to comb whatever the queen
bee says to.

Ducks are not caring where they lay their eggs so until they do don't let them go swiming. Or above you.

I understand how the chicks get out of their shells, but how they get in who knows.

I have never seen a cowbird so I don't know which is which half.

Pigs like to be clean. They try to do it by rolling in the mud, not being as smart as we.

Barn swallows, naturally, have rather large mouths.

A parakeet is a friendly bird. He will eat seeds or your hand.

Many parrots (as well as humans) have the custom of matting for life. They are said to be insufferable.

We found many mother baby hamsters were often grandmothers by the time they were four months old. But then we watched how they were fast livers.

Gorillas are always fighting. You hear talk all the time about gorilla warfare.

(*Is the kangaroo peculiar to Australia?*)
No, but it sure is to us.

CHAPTER 4

Brave New Electronic World

Many things that were once thought to be science fiction now actually are."

A child of our dawning space age wrote that in a classroom essay recently, and I was startled by the truth of it. This little boy had summed up in a sentence some of the most fantastic progress ever made by man . . . his spaceships, his satellites, and his rockets to probe the far reaches of the solar system.

When I was a boy, my hero was Buck Rogers, the invincible spaceman of the comic pages. But now spaceships have soared out of the fantasy of the comics into the headlines of reality. Flesh and blood heroes like Colonel John Glenn have orbited

an astonished earth and one day will be landing on the moon. Even old Buck's ray gun is being perfected in the laboratories, as scientists continue to master the energies of light.

The world of kids has changed, too, since my generation learned to read and write. The little red schoolhouse has all but disappeared, and with it the old pot-bellied stove that stood in the corner, and the rows of desks with initials and valentine hearts carved all over them. Schools built today have air conditioning, scientific lighting, motion pictures and TV.

It all *seems* so different—but the kids themselves haven't changed at all. They may talk about their model jet planes and atomic submarines at recess, but they're still struggling the same way their mothers and fathers did to see the grown-up world right side up.

How are our kids doing at understanding the complex theories of modern science, atomic energy, nuclear fission, and the like? Let's ask them and see! Here's one boy's explanation of atomic fission:

"See there are these electrons and protons that are on opposite sides of the atom. They meet and fight it out. When things get hottest and the atom can't stand it any more, it explodes."

Another boy wrote this:

"I think I admire the electron more than anything else about the atom because it weighs only about one over 2000th as much as a proton but can still hold its own."

If you're a little behind on your modern physics, this student's explanation may help:

"Electrons carry the negative charge while the protons provide the affirmative."

That's right! (I'm positive.) And here's something I never knew before:

"Inside every molecule are many, many Adams."

Here's a new slant on an old saying:

"With the coming of the atom, we know now what was meant when it was said 'the pen is mightier than the sword.' The period about to end this sentence for just one thing has zillions of unexploded atoms in it."

How would you describe a vacuum? Here's one child's answer, brief and exact:

"A vacuum is an empty place with nothing to it."

The vast emptiness of space awed another boy into writing this:

"There is no air in space. That means there is nothing. Try to think of it. It is easier to think of anything than nothing."

The fun comes when a kid scores a near miss on the target of knowledge and comes up with a genuine blooper:

"Many broken windows result from masonic booms."

Often a grownup can only envy the simplicity and beauty of a child's way of expression, as in the case of the girl who wrote that "Climate is with us all the time while weather comes and goes."

Perfectly true, isn't it?

A very young poet wrote this:

"The wind is like the air, only pushier."

Sometimes the kids develop novel theories of their own. A boy who evidently rebelled against those Saturday night baths in chilly weather thought of this idea:

"We should not take our bath in winter as often as in summer. If we will only let our clothes and us get a little darker, we take in the heat from the sun better."

There are even times when a child does learn his lessons, but can't fit them together properly. One indignant lad wrote a note to his physics teacher, saying:

"You told me warm air rises, and then you said the higher you go, the colder it gets. Which may I believe?"

Think *that* one over awhile!

Let's go wandering now through the whole field of science and find out what our kids have learned —or think they've learned:

While molecules in gases and liquids bounce around
   from place to place, in solids they just lay there
   and vibrate.

Cotton is used to make clothes and gin.

Hi fi has made radio singers a lot more faithful.

How to tell when spring is here is you can look for
bears. Too, birds flying backside from the south.

(*Why are days shorter in winter than in summer?*)
During the cold winter months, the days get
cold and contract. In the summer time they get
hot and expand.

Rain clouds float around up there and then they bump
into each other and out falls the rain.

A hurricane has an eye in it. This is like a cycclops.

Someday a man will go to the moon. This is a loony
orbit.

You never know how rockets will behave because
they go through stages.

Tides are interesting if you happen to be interested in them.

The earth holds on to everything with its grabity.

Newton noticed that anything at rest tended to remain at rest. For this he grew famous.

(*What does the inertial law of Galileo prove?*)
That there are some things I don't know.

You can listen to thunder after lightning and tell how
close you came to geting hit. If you don't hear it
then you got hit, so never mind.

In taking the word indivisible, we have an interesting one. Altho America (since the Civil War) is
indivisible, the atoms in America (since 1945)

have been divisible. Atoms in Russia and England and other countries are also becoming no longer indivisible. Remember this is not to say they are invisible (altho they are). This is to say something else.

Evaporated is things we can't see like evaporated milk.

Light travels faster in hot weather than it does in cold. In the summer it gets here before 6:00.

Heated air moves faster but so would we all.

You can cook things with charcoal by putting it in brassieres. Women wear other kinds to keep warm also.

(*Why does a compass always point North?*)
They are stubborn that way.

We have to send light through a prison before it will show all its colors.

(*What do stratus clouds look like?*)
Rain.

Molecules are constantly bumping around each other in the air. There is really quite an overpopulation of molecules.

Protons are found mainly in meat and electricity.

(*Why is the flame extinguished when a bottle is
placed over the candle?*)
Because of Magic.

One of the most important things to remember about
clouds is oh I forget what I started to say.

Gravity is caused because objects and bodies and
things attract each other to them. Opposites
especially, and in electricity and people.

If you are in a boat and want to stop, the best way is
to dig your pole in the bottom of the river.
Friction can always stop you this way even if
the boat goes on.

Water vapor gets together in a cloud. When it is big
enough to be called a drop it does.

Each light bulb contains many whats. We don't know
for sure yet.

Two great forces are constantly opposing each other.
They are known as gravity and the centrifical

force. There will always be wars and rumors of wars as long as these two forces are allowed to exist.

The four seasons are the best ones I know of.

High up in the sky the air is very thin. It is only close to the ground that we find the fat kind.

We can expect rain most when the pressure is feeling low. It is in the sunshine that we are most apt to be high.

Most metals are definately more or less elastic.

Ball bearings and plenty of oil are needed for a machine to osculate properly.

Since they have learned that whirlpools are not caused by demons, sailors caught in them can now know it is not demons that killed them.

(*What's the difference between a bolt and a nut?*)
A bolt is a thing like a stick of hard metal such as iron with a square bunch on one end and a lot of scratching wound around the other end. A nut is similar to the bolt only just the opposite, being a hole in a little chunk of iron, sawed off short, with wrinkles around the inside of the hole.

The highest of all clouds are the circus clouds.

We think the earth feels still but it is in a constant commotion going around itself.

Hail comes in all sizes but not for long.

Slush is snow with all the fun melted out.

Rain is saved up in cloud banks.

Fish can drown in air. That is true. So we are even.

CHAPTER 5

Cleopatria Loves Mark (Twain)

How the great men of history would laugh, if only they could return to earth and see themselves the way our modern school kids think of them. I can just picture America's great humorist, Mark Twain, holding his sides and doubling up at the thought of being remembered by one junior historian as the "Mark" who was the lover of Cleopatra. Twain knew a lot more about Mississippi rafts than he ever did about barges on the Nile . . . but come to think of it, I'll bet that the author of *Huckleberry Finn* would have enjoyed a Nile cruise with Queen Cleo.

History is like one big fairy-tale storybook to our younger school kids. Not until high school can we expect them to have any real understanding of the vast sweep of history through the centuries. Instead, the little ones visualize history as a series of fanciful tales about famous heroes, leaders and adventurers. They have little notion of how very long ago it was that Caesar's legions campaigned through Gaul or Hannibal came marching over the Alps. Being so very new on earth themselves, kids figure that anybody who lived before their grandparents were born must have been very old indeed. Young minds have a way of losing count as they try to roll the years backward to the days of Alexander the Great, who impressed one admiring student as being "one of my favorite tirants."

Perhaps the Italian explorer who discovered America might be somewhat upset to read one young skeptic's verdict on him:

"I don't believe Columbus is as famous as most people think he is."

But I'm sure that President Lincoln would laugh to hear that he was nicknamed "Honest Ape" because he was a good man, but homely.

There are times when a child hits closer to the truth than he realizes, as when a boy observed:

"Despite her fighting leadership, most historians agree that Joan of Arc was really a tinder woman."

Anybody who has struggled with geometry can enjoy the unintentional humor in this one:

"Phethagerous wrote down many things about geometry that man should know for his own good.

We were very fortunate to have him living for such a short time."

Let's run through the alphabet of some of our best known historical figures; I guarantee you'll find things out that you never "knew" before:

ADAM and EVE wore nothing but figments.

JOHN ADAMS was actually not his son, so he put a Quincy in between his son so we would know.

ANESTHESIA was the last of the Russian princesses.

(*Who was JOHNNY APPLESEED?*)

A man famous for scattering his seed all over the country.

BENEDICT ARNOLD was a trader. He traded sides.

ALEXANDER GRAHAM BELL invented the telephone. We named the telephone bell after him.

WILLIAM BENDIX invented the automatic washer.

IRVING BERLIN composes both the words and lyrics of his songs.

JOHN BROWN was caught by the south and executed in 1859. No I take that back, he was hung.

WILLIAM JENNINGS BRYANT was nominated for president in three different Democratic Convents.

(*What did JULIUS CAESAR write?*)
Latin.

(*Name a famous woman scientist.*)
KATE CANAVERAL.

ROBINSON CARUSO was a great singer, unfortunately shipwrecked.

CLEOPATRIA was a wicked ruler. She was just like
Julius Caesar except the wrong sex only moreso.

By getting to be president, CLEVELAND reached
the pinochle of success. A first name for him
was Grover.

LEON CZOLGOSZ shot the gun that fatally killed
President McKinley.

RICHARD DANA sailed around the horn to California and tanned a lot of hides.

(*Who was DEMOSTHENES?*)

He was a great talker who practiced with a mouth of pebbles. It really works and you can try it with bubblegum.

(*Describe DEMOSTHENES.*)

I have never seen any of these.

THOMAS EDISON invented the lightbulb because he needed it. He didn't sleep much.

My favorite American was BEN FRANKLIN because here is why. He worked hard & thought a lot & soforth.

It is not true, the story of BEN FRANKLIN flying his kite in a thunderstorm. Only a nut would try it.

GALILEO proved beyond a doubt that heavy things and light ones fall at the same speed. Of course the world has changed since then.

If GENERAL GRANT'S formula for success could be summed up in one sentence, it would be this: Always start everything you finish.

GULLIBLE was the traveler.

HAMLET was a small pig made famous by Shakespear.

HANNIBAL had a lot of elephants. He charged them at the enemy.

HANNIBAL had a great stroke of luck in his march toward Rome. For if the Alps had not happened to be there, he would never have been able to cross them.

What made O. HENRY so unusual was he wasn't really who his name said he was.

❖
❖ ❖
❖

Today we know HOMER was not one but several people. Some say some Homers might even be from other countries but they all seem Greek to me.

Both sides of ALDOUS HUXLEY were well edu-
cated.

When THOMAS JEFFERSON was getting ready to
retire, they held a banquet to give him a little
momentum.

EDWARD JENNER taught us that if there is a lot
of sickness going around, we should go get a
shot of something.

JOSEPH didn't wear bathrobes like other men in the
   Bible. He liked sports coats and had one of
   many colors.

I know of only one person smarter than president
   KENNEDY. Can you think who? Sure! Or at
   least that is who I would say.

LAVOISIER was the inventor of mouth wash.

PETER LAWFORD is a good friend of President
   Kennedy who is also the lady he is married to's
   brother.

HENRY LONGFELLOW is one of our most famous
   bookmakers.

MACADAM was the first Scotchman.

MAGELLAN sailed all the way around the world where he discovered geography.

MARCONI invented the noodle and stuff like that.

CYRUS McCORMICK invented the grim reaper.

ISSAC NEWTON passed the law of gravity.

PLASTER OF PARIS makes dress fashions.

WILEY POST had only his left eye due to an accident. Or maybe it was his right no it must have oh why does it matter so much?

SIR WALTER RALEIGH was a rich sailor with a golden hind.

Whether WILLIAM SHAKESPEARE really wrote all his plays is not certain. It is thought by some that they might have been written by a William Shakespeare, the Different, another man by the same name.

The abominable SNOWMAN is called that because he won't let people shoot him.

STALIN has now been discredited by removing his esophagus.

ST. CHRISTOPHER always looks after travelers unless they go too fast.

In just a few short years MARK TWAIN became a sensation overnight.

GEORGE WASHINGTON is one of my favorites like when he didn't let the British know he was

out of bulits but kept firing. I read many things on him in a book. It was a brown one for 14 days. I am glad he comes but once a year.

WHISTLER'S was the dearest mother he had.

CHAPTER 6

General Custard and Daniel Boom

SPECIALISTS are supposed to be experts who know more and more about less and less. Kids are just the opposite, because they know almost nothing about everything. Only a kid could sum up the entire history of the United States in one magnificently inadequate phrase: "In American history, there was first Columbus, then on to now." Only a child could make such a merry slip as this: "The American Revolution was caused by taxation without relaxation." On the other hand, maybe that last boy was right! We might all be British subjects today if King George had only relaxed a little on that tea tax.

Here's one pint-sized patriot's version of how we drummed King George's Redcoats out of our colonies:

"The british thought they were so smart they at-
tacked us all over. But we showed them. Ha Ha.
There was no use there trying to outfight us because
we were right. After we showed them, they got out
so we could have the forth of july."

The Father of our Country seemed all too virtuous
to one little doubter who wrote:

"George Washington never told a lie and I don't
believe it."

Here are some little-known facts from the days of
the Civil War:

"One reason the South lost the war was they made
Confederate money, not knowing it was worthless."

"Lincoln was setting in a theater booth when he
was killed. It was John Wilke's booth."

"Lincoln soon proved to be mortally wounded by the shot, as was the nation, to a lesser degree."

"Honest Abe got that nickname because he had been taught so that he would not do anything, and even if he did not to sneak around the bush about it if asked."

If you're a Western history fan, you may be surprised to read these rather original ideas on the pioneer days:

"Rawhide saddles were called that because that is how they made you."

"Covered wagons were often used in rum-running. This is why they kept them covered."

Now let's follow a trail of very small footsteps into America's past, and see what our school kids have to say about the growth of the USA:

All of our ancestors were not born in America but came from other places. As a mattery fact, some of us might be surprised to learn where we came from.

Columbus called the people Indians because everybody thought they were in India. We still do even to this day.

We don't know who lost New York in the first place but Peter Sylverson founded it again somewhere among the 16 hundreds.

(*Where did our pioneers come from?*)
I am not sure but I know it is not the stork.

While stagecoaches carried both kind of passengers, the pony express would only carry the male.

Once upon a time Gorge Washington had a birthday. And his father gave him a shinny new ax. And Gorge took it outside and started chopping a stowt cherry tree. Yes! And his father came home and looked at what he had done. Yes! So he asked Gorge and Gorge said he had, and that is all.

After the war, Washington perferred to retire to his rusty home in Mt. Vernon.

The pioneers prided themselves on their clean homes. Even if they only had dirt floors it was never a dirty kind.

The men of colonial days were gentlemen, and there ladies were grand dames.

Those men at the California missions who wore long robes were called "monks," so the ladies who worked with them must have been "monkeys."

King George decided he didn't want us to have our
   freedom. I don't know why not but it wasn't a
   very good reason.

What the settlers settled were fusses before civilaza-
   tion came to us.

In the older days the cowboies main job was to take
   care of the cows. Also the bad Engines.

The invention of the handcar made it possible for man to travel by hand as well as by foot.

(*What is a boom town?*)
A town settled by Daniel Boom.

"The Spirit of 76" is talking about 76 ghosts thought up to scare the Bridish.

Pioneers razed mostly crops and houses.

When they had sheep, the pinears made their cloths from sheep wool. When they had no sheep, they got their wool from bufalos and other wild animals. This was harder.

Blunderbuses represented the first crude attempt to travel mechanically.

The West used to be full of cowboys but they all shot each other.

Frontier women made their own colors for killing or rather dieing their clothes.

Every U.S. Cavalryman was trained to be brave. If he was scalped, he was never to show it.

In the old days they had good indians and bad indians. The bad indians were the ones who shot
back.

The apaches raised the roof with the settlers.

The Pony Express was a system worked out to send
ponies through the mail.

The Civil War was a threat to the unity of the Untied
States.

(*Would you rather be Davy Crockett or General
Grant? Why?*)
I don't care. Either way I am dead.

The Indians liked to scallop their victims.

General Custer was killed in the Battle of Little Big
Horn. This proved to be his undoing.

Little Big Horn sounds as confusing to me as to
General Custard.

The Civil War is because we acted Kind and Civil to
each other since we were all Americans. Like
no shooting in the back if you have Kings X.
And no fair throwing mud.

It was October '29 when it finally happened. With the crash of the markets, valuable stocks became invaluable overnight.

Unfortunately, the depression happened just as everybody was out of work.

When a cowboy got a group of horses together, he would put them in a chorale.

John Kennedy is my favorite 34th president of the United States.

(*Who said, "If this be treason, make the most of it"?*)
Benedict Arnold.

(*What did France give the United States for New York harbor?*)
I don't know. I thought it was still ours.

To get the gold out of the water, the California miners used a river bedpan.

The Puritans came to this country so they could enjoy freedom of persecution.

(*Who is the First Lady?*)
Eve.

The early colonists punished people by taking them to the market and putting them into stocks.

In the winter, if the pioneers found any sugar-maple
trees, they would send somebody out in the cold
to get his. Then they would get the sap and boil
him in syrup and sugar. I know this sounds
cruel, but times were hard then.

Franklin Roosevelt was the longest president we
ever had.

(*What happened at the Battle of the Alamo?*)
We lost.

When the Indians got together, they held their bow wows.

The President says we should not send any gold drains overseas.

CHAPTER 7

Martians, Meteors and Moonshine

Twinkle, twinkle, little star,
How I wonder what you are,
Up above the world so high,
Like a diamond in the sky.

IMAGINE YOURSELF a child again on some balmy
summer evening, gazing upward at those mysterious, twinkling diamonds in the sky. You feel as if
you could almost reach on tiptoe to touch them, and
yet your teacher has told you that they are millions
of miles away. The stories you hear at school about
the universe seem more fantastic than any of the
bedtime tales that mother used to read to you.

Teacher says that the world is really a round ball
. . . that it spins entirely around each day . . . that
it's rushing through space in a vast orbit around the
sun . . . and that there are millions of other "suns" in
the far, galactic depths beyond. These are ideas that
you must take on faith, because your mind cannot
grasp the immensities of the universe. So you come
away from your starry communion, feeling the same
kind of awe that humans have always felt since the
time they first raised their eyes to the heavens.

Looking at the universe as the kids sometimes see
it is like looking through the wrong end of a tele-
scope . . . but it's fun to try! Only a kid could dream
up a theory such as this one about the possibility of
life on the moon:

"While going around the earth, the moon also turns
around itself once. Since it has learned how to turn
around itself, this makes me know there is higher in-
telligents on the moon."

They say there aren't many people who really understand Einstein's theory of relativity . . . but here's
a new version of it that seems to make a sense all its
own:

"When things heaten they expand. Our expanding
universe, just as a case, is caused by our increasing
hot summers."

One of the dizziest, mind-spinning attempts to
link up one fact with another that I've ever read was

a boy's thought about weightlessness in outer space:

"Col. Glen flew so fast he didn't weigh anything. But when he slowed down he weighed like his old self again. This explains maybe why fat people are so heavy, is because they go slower than other people."

Many centuries ago, a primitive tribe in India believed that the earth was a huge tea tray, supported on the backs of three giant elephants which in turn were standing on the shell of an enormous tortoise. Just as fanciful were the ancient Egyptians, who thought the sky was a heavenly Nile where the great sun god, Ra, went sailing every day from dawn until dusk. Today there are no longer believers in celestial tea trays, although flying saucers are still popular. There are even some diehards around who believe the world is flat . . . so perhaps we shouldn't be surprised when kids are skeptical about science:

"The earth is moving through space at a terrific speed, circling the sun while the moon circles us. At least this is the latest theory."

"The Nebulus Theory of how the earth got started is still pretty hazy."

"If we could only believe what we read, the sun would be a million miles more times farther than the earth."

The vast distances of interplanetary space dazzled one student into writing this:

"Marz is so far off it takes a million years to walk there on an express train."

Another boy thought it was just as well that Mars *was* so far away, pointing out that:

"It is just as far for the Marsians to get to us as we to get to them, so we have that constillation."

Here are more ideas on the moon, meteors, and miscellany:

I have read where some say the moon is too hot too live on. Others say it is too cold. So I bet it's just right.

When meteors strike our air it burns them up. Luckly air effects we of the humans unlike that.

To anyone on the moon, they would look and think the earth is only just a mirror for the sun, so that shows how much they know.

One reason for getting to Mars is that people live
longer there. Say like a man is 100 years here
on Earth, well he is much less older on Mars. It
sounds crazy but it is so.

There is one side of the moon we have never looked
at. I am not for sure exactly which side it is.

For as long as the moon has been there, it has made
a trip around the earth every month. There is
not much else to do.

We have never been able to see but one side of the moon. No one has ever seen the inside yet.

Life in outer space is much different from what we usually hear. Listen. ?????. What did I say? Search me. You see this shows we are unable to hear anything like a sound in outer space.

The planets traveling around the sun are all part of our Sonar System.

When we see the sitting sun at night it does not really move. We are the ones that move and sit.

I understand about day and night but it takes me longer to think out winter and summer. It takes the sun about 365 days.

Night is when we get on the shady side of the sun.

Clouds are what make the moon move when you watch it.

The "moon" is really a satellite. But I and a lot of other people still catch ourselves calling it "moon."

Jupiter has twelve moons circling around it. It has a lot of pull, you see.

Some people can tell what time it is by looking at
the sun, but I have never been able to make out
the numbers.

The moon follows our earth in a circle or bit.

(*Where is Mercury?*)
It hides in thermometers.

It happens to take the earth one year exactly to go around the sun.

A trip to the moon would take longer than I would care to take the time to figure out.

(*In what ways are we dependent upon the sun?*)
    We can always depend on the sun for sunburns and tidal waves.

(*Why is the sky blue?*)
    Because when sunlight hits the air it bends a little, this being the right answer to one of the questions, this one I think.

Space scientists call outer space that. This is as good a name as I can think for it.

❖
❖ ❖
❖

Now that we know that planets are made of rocks and stars are made of gases, all we have to do is get close enough to tell which.

In the light of the moon on a clear night is the best time to get all the moonshine possible.

In order to know that the moon has gravity I need only look at the tides. Somehow this proves it to me concluesively.

Some claim how days and nights on the moon are two weeks old. This makes for good talk and who can prove different?

The moon means more to us than the sun because it shines at night when we need it most.

Our nights our not as cold on earth as on other planets. If so our plants and animals could not live. Us either.

When we mention the sun we are really talking about a star. And when we say stars we should really say suns. We will know why after we explore them.

Everybody leans to the sun in summer and away in winter. We are all a little tipsy that way.

To think that snowflakes fall from the stars is crazy. We all learn that snowflakes have *six* points.

While the sun continues to reklessly fly through space, we blindly follow along and around it. But some day we will learn how to go on our own and then watch out.

Through the years people have guessed that Venus
  might be inhabited by women, dragons, or other
  strange creatures.

Water really has oxygen just like we breathe, but
  don't try it.

Saturn looks better with a few belts.

The air keeps the sun from burning us, but smart
  people rub some stuff on themselves in summer
  just the same.

The air is miles thick, but most thick on the ground. Humans are better at having thick air.

There is a new moon every month, but we only say that. Really it is the same old moon every time.

(*Describe the water cycle.*)
The water cycle is a thing on which one or more persons can ride on the water by petaling along. I don't believe it has been invented yet.

CHAPTER 8

The Pharaohs and Their Mommies

ONE OF THE best cartoon shows for kids on television has been "The Flintstones," an imaginative series about a cave man and his family who have all the modern comforts—a stone TV set, a telephone made from a conch shell, and even a pedal-powered automobile. What fascinates me about the show is that grownups laugh at the idea of a cave man enjoying a twentieth century life . . . but our little kids seem to take it for granted. After all, why shouldn't cave kids be watching TV as they do themselves? Why shouldn't their mothers gossip on the phone, and fix dinner in kitchens with stoves and refrigerators? A cave like that makes far more sense than the ones that our archeologists tell us were inhabited in prehistoric times by beetle-browed, club-swinging characters who wore animal skins.

History for kids is a merry mix-up of the ancient and the modern, a timeless stage where kings and conquerors, heroes and warriors come and go with little regard for the centuries. Little boys and girls who can barely tell time by the clock can hardly be expected to remember whether it was Hannibal or Napoleon who had those elephants—or which man came first.

Just for fun, let's read some history as our children see it, starting with some comments on man's earliest days on earth:

"In cave man times they all had odd names like Alley Oop and Homo Sapiens."

"I am suspicious that there were smart-as-human creatures before humans ourselves. For one thing, I know there were no humans alive during the Mesozoic period, but someone was still there to name it."

"We know human beings lived as long as one-million years ago since we have found trash and ashes in the one-million year ago earth layer. We know only humans could have made this mess."

"Man has been on the earth for only a drop in the bucket."

By the time we move on to ancient Egypt, the confusion is deepening:

"The people in Egyptian times invented 365 days in a year, but true democrasies refined it by sticking in an extra day every four years for elections."

"The pyramids are so far out from any place, getting to them is said to be one of the seven great wanders of the world."

I'd love to have seen the teacher's reaction in this question-and-answer exchange:

Did the Sumerians, Egyptians or Hittites live closest to the Nile River?

False.

It's certainly true, as one pupil wrote, that "foreign history is getting longer and harder all the time." But if our kids don't know all the answers, they can always do what their parents once did . . . try to slide by on a guess or two:

"Gaul was called that because it's people had so much of it."

"The Roman Legends were Legends soldiers went around telling about how great Rome was."

"The Romans are called that by History because they never stayed in one place."

Here are some of my favorite questions and answers:

When were the Middle Ages?

Somewhere around 40rty.

When was the Age of Discovery?
   For me about 9.

Name the major European sport of the 18th century.
   Casanova.

Let's continue with history you didn't know till now:

The moon calendar of the early people proved to be
   wrong because what if it was a cloudy night?

People first shook hands to prove they had no arms.
   That is, of course, they could keep their flesh
   and boney kind.

An achronism is an impossible thing of the past. As for the future, no one can say for sure.

For centuries, man wondered what a missing link might look like. Finally someone figured out that it wasn't worth the trouble in knowing anyway.

A floating population is like when they found baby Moses in the bulls rushes.

Though I hear about them all the time, I have never knowingly seen a holy roaming empire.

July is called after Julius Caesar. One day he decided, "you know I would like another month of summer," and that is how it happened.

Althouh the Greeks and Romans lived pretty close together on the map and learned a lot from each other and did many things alike and looked a lot alike, there the resemblance ends.

All the Pharaohs wanted to be mommies. It usually killed them.

As soon as the Romes captured the Europeons they started presecuting them. So every body hated them. Pretty soon the Romes changed their mind and had good people and built good roads and other things and so every body still hated them.

Sometimes we think of the Persians as living when the world was younger. At other times it is the old or ancient times. It depends mosty on where you count from.

In ancient times, crimes were called aniquities and good deeds were antiquities.

Things got so bad in the dark ages that monks were smarter than humans.

(*When was the Magna Carta signed?*)
At 12:15.

The good that knights did was they brought loin order to the land. They would not stand for meanness but stood for curage.

One cause of progress slowing up is when barbarian chiefs pass the power to their children and then on down to their children without letting the grownups run it.

As we learned about printing books and how to have liesure and everything, knowledge and man spread wider and wider.

The French Revolution was fermented by the middle classes.

As Napoleon was backing through Russia he must have realized all his dreams had been for nougat.

The Bore War was a very dull one.

I am not speaking to Khruschef.

Knights always carried a coat of arms with them. I forget what they used them for, but they remembered and that was what was important.

(*Where was the treaty ending the First World War
     signed?*)
     On page 117.

Humanity can gain a great lesson from the world
     war number two, although historians are the
     only ones who know for sure what it is.

The Knights of old fought for ladys hankerchiefs and
     stockings and other favors they got.

(*What great event occurred in 1066?*)
     That was so long ago that I don't remember.

Eskimos enjoy blubbering at every meal.

The Irish have very heavy brogans.

One of the wisest of all Romans came from Cincinnati.

The Greeks made wonderful statues. They were the best chiselers of the ancient world.

The Egyptians lived before money so they used sediment which they deposited in the banks of the Nile.

SEDIMENTAL JOURNEY

The Franks invented the wiener.

The Saturnalia was the time when all the Romans took their baths.

In the old days, all countries were run by kings, queens and jacks.

(*Name a great leader of the Crusades.*)
Eisenhower.

In the Middle Ages, knights had fun knocking each other off horses. This was called jesting.

CHAPTER 9

Money Can Make You Rich

BACK IN MY OWN boyhood days, a kid had to be a shrewd trader to survive in a world of junior financiers who knew exactly how much the current baseball picture cards were worth on the bubble gum market. These were the same sharpies who would trade you out of your best aggies, or lure you into a game for keeps where you'd lose all your marbles to the big boys. Sometimes a windfall might come along to refinance your operations, such as an unexpected find of pop bottles that could be redeemed for cash at the corner grocery. But usually we kids learned our first lessons in economics the hard way, discovering soon enough that careless traders go home with empty pockets.

118

The economics of the grown-up world aren't really so very different. Our stock exchanges are basically places where men can trade stocks for whatever they think they're worth, just as they once traded pictures of Babe Ruth and Ty Cobb. And if a man insists on flinging his marbles away on a good time, there's always Las Vegas or Reno.

The fun comes when kids try to understand how the adult system of economics operates. One boy gave this encouraging tip on how to grow prosperous:

"Stocks and bonds and all those things are not always necessary. Many people have struck it rich with little more than money."

A future conservative wrote this:

"Our country's national prosperity is exceeded only by our national debt."

If you've never quite understood why the stock market crashed in the 20's, this kid's theory comes very close to the truth:

"1929 happened because people kept putting their savings in stocks instead of money."

Kids know about taxes, too:

"A surtax is the tax put on high gentlemen."

"Income tacks are the most expensive kind."

A future Bernard Baruch evidently wrote this:

"Bartering means trading for something you don't have for something the other person doesn't have.

But of course if you really don't have it and he doesn't either, you can see why people had to invent money before things got to compleacated."

Here's something for the people in Washington to think about:

"Post offices often mark over our stamps so we can't possibly use them again. This is a good example of the government waste we hear about."

There are times when a kid says more than he realizes, as these did:

"Much of the work of the government has been trained to be done by civil serpents."

"We now live in the Age of Steal."

Social studies classes are the soil where such boners sprout up, so let's wander at random through the whole field and pick some more favorites:

Life insurance makes it possible so that if a man dies he will have something after he dies for we know he cannot take anything along made while living.

One result of inflation is that ten pennies are now worth only one dime.

It is the duty of the legislature to confine the presidents appointees.

Two ways to prevent floods are to plant trees and damn the streams. It is hard work.

Only in wars and epidemics does our country ask
  us to bear our arms.

"For the benefit of mankind" means to think of your
  children. Or if you don't have any, then your
  children's children and theirs and on as far as
  you can think.

(*When is our next presidential election to be held?*)
  By and by.

The president keeps all his secretaries in a cabinet.

Our Four Freedoms are: Freedom from Want, Freedom from Fear, Freedom from the Press and Freedom from Religion.

I am positive there will never be another world war, will there?

Post office workers are called clerks and carriers but not like diseases or anything like that.

If you want to vote on something, you can always get up a partition.

Too many Americans think only about television sets and automobiles and other such frivlious necessities.

Dictators are mean and people who want to be them are too. If anybody ever asked me if I wanted to be a dictator, I could truthfully say no, yes no! in answering.

In order to be certain of having a house for a long period of time, the house should be leashed.

It takes an act of Congress to make an officer a gentleman.

Many consider our nation's no. 1 problem to be jubilant delinquency.

Compared to a General, a Kernel's pay is just chicken-feed.

Many law inforcing officers say that walkers should be given tickets just like drivers when they disobey the law. It is for their own safeness. I hardily agree.

To have faith in your convictions means no matter how many times you go to jail you know it's for your own good.

Capital punishment should not be used in the training of little children.

One good thing about the king system over the presidents is many of them have the same first name so all you have to remember is what comes after VII, VIII, X and the like.

No property can change hands without first everyone sinning on the dotted line.

A Representative is somebody who is very average.

Politicians kiss babies to get votes. This is gooey
work.

UNESCO is a kind of cookie.

The good kind of ministers are in church, and the
other kind are in government.

The Red Cross ladies are always ready to offer themselves for charity.

After criminals go to jail, the best ones are let out
first.

In the old days, men walked on the outside of women so they wouldn't get dirty.

Now that women can vote, they have bigger seats in everything.

When a man and woman are married a long time, they form a strong detachment.

Every ten years we count our census. Five the last time.

Everybody ought to give juvenile delinquency a helping hand.

CHAPTER 10

From Hawaya to
Belchum

TODAY'S KIDS have a magic carpet called television that whisks them away on exciting adventures to exotic places all over the world. Long before they're old enough to go to school, they're already pushing through the jungles on safaris, striding the decks of South Seas schooners, or exploring the ocean depths with the aquanauts. Movies, travelogues and adventure shows are their first lessons in what the rest of the globe and its peoples are like.

Besides enjoying these imaginary journeys via TV, modern boys and girls are much more traveled in real life than their mothers and fathers ever were. It's become an American custom to pack the kids into the family car and go places when vacation time

129

comes along. Some fortunate families even fly off to Hawaii or Europe, as only the prosperous few once did.

With all this knowledge and experience behind them, kids find that geography can be fun. As one boy said, "Geography is good because it lets us go places. Even if we had already been there it is still fun. Once upon a time I visited Mexico and thanks to geography I can revisit it again if I ever want to."

Here's something to feel thankful for:

"Only about ¼ of the world is land. America is lucky to be mainly on this ¼ dry part."

Or, as another boy who was a little more concerned about it said, "While we spend all our time worrying about Russia, more than ⅔ of the world remains under water."

Perhaps those two students were thinking of the fate of the legendary Atlantis, which a boy defined as "a continent somebody misplaced thousands of years ago."

Let's take a trip with our junior geographers, and see what they've mapped out in their minds:

Hawaya is a relaxed state and people do nothing mostly except sit and sway and palm trees too.

Belchum is found in between France and Germany on most maps.

Weather they live in Northern or Southern Poland, the Poles have the coldest spots on earth.

One of the most unusual sights in Italy is a leaning tower of pizza.

Population is thickening steadily in the lumbar regions of Canada.

The globe comes to a point as you reach either pole because everything shrinks in the cold.

I think our state is the most beautiful in the whole country. Of course I may be a little pregnant.

The Antarctic is like the regular arctic, but ritzier.

Canada and Australia have several things in common. For one they are both in the Common Wealth and for another they are both far apart.

Although America is spread rather thin in other places, it is good and thick in the Rocky Mountain area.

It used to be thought that we had 48 states in America. Then someone counted again and there was 50.

New York is better than Los Angeles because you can get out of school there sometimes. Los Angeles don't have blizzards or snow or anything swell like that.

The Mississippi River is very important to us so that we will have a way to get from one side to another.

The great plains are called that because they are so flat that even the largest plains can land there.

While passing through Kansas, a typhoon is really not a hurricane but a tornado.

There is hardly any winter in Miami. They passed a law or something.

More people live in Road Island than is possible.

Some parts of the Grand Canyon are a mile deep and two miles high.

It can most of the time be said that it never rains in California.

I am sorry I don't know about the high Sierras, or how they got that high.

East of New York, it has been found that railroad travel is faster by boat.

Although there was once no water in the Gulf of Mexico, the people who named it somehow knew that water was coming.

Greece is just a little spot on the map.

Argentina people are not called Argentines. Their pronunciation is some-what different. They pronounce themselves Argentenians.

(*Why did Magellan travel completely around the world?*)
Because.

Mesopotamia was located between the Tigeress and the deep blue Euphrates.

In Africa they write messages on their dum dums.

Sailors have learned never to start across the Pacific in anything that weighs more than the Pacific Gravity.

An arroyo is a deep place hallowed by wind and rain.

A kindly climate is one where the weather is nice to you.

When any place has an earthquake, guess what caused it? That is as good a guess as anybodie's since no one knows for sure.

There are no directions at the North Pole, but there is no place up there to go anyhow.

As the Arabian Arabs wandered threw the hot vast-less desert they came upon a strange tree that

grew there by itself which is one thing that made it such a strange tree.

By learning that Krakston is located between Sumatra and Java, I now know three places I can look for instead of just one.

In France the word for seven is sept. One day they will think and see it should be july.

Some of my directions I get confused as exampled in N is from W left no right no up no S no E, so see?

Men who know have figured out that if Mt. Everest was thrown into the deep downmost part of the ocean it would all be under water, so we know not to go to all the trouble.

The Colorado River is harnessed by a Hoover D—.

Ships can take a shortcut through the Sewage Canal if they are in that much of a hurry.

When it is day in America it is night in China. They are a backward country.

Wives cost a lot of money in Africa. They aren't worth anything here.

The high lamas of Tibet have long silky hair.

Oxford is where they make a low type of shoe.

Until the missionaries came, the cannibals ate each other.

(*What was the Colossus of Rhodes?*)
    Route 66?

The Swiss people are always yodeling and ringing bells. Other people have let them be for hundreds of years.

The people in Holland believe in storks.

The country of the Amazons is full of wild women.

People in Spain take naps every afternoon. This is called a sombrero.

It is so hot that the natives wear very few clothes in the Spicy Islands.

The Shetland Islands are in the Horse Latitudes.

Food can be grown in dry areas if you irritate the land.

(*What do we call the land Down Under?*)
Dirt, mostly.

Latitude is so we can travel straight across the world instead of just up and down.

(*Where are the Appalachian Mountains?*)
Right there on the map.

The French people drink wine but they used to have some famous Bourbons.

The Solomon islands are full of wise old men.

The Swiss people are quite high and the Dutch are the lowest.

The Chinese like rotten eggs and make soup from birds nests. They can have it.

California is a great place to visit, but I wouldn't want to leave there.

CHAPTER *11*

Hearts Are for Valentines

What are little boys made of?
Snips and snails, and puppy-dogs' tails;
That's what little boys are made of.
What are little girls made of?
Sugar and spice, and everything nice;
That's what little girls are made of.

NEXT TO THE all-important question of where he
came from, a child seems to be fascinated most by
what he's made of. He learns very early in life what
his eyes and ears and hands and feet are for, but
soon he begins wondering about his insides . . . his
brain, his heart, his stomach, and all the rest of those
mysterious innards that his parents say he has.

One of my own favorite lines is a kid's definition of
a spinal column:

"The spine is a bunch of bones. Your head sits on one end and you sit on the other."

That's plain enough, but here's another about bones that's sure to slow you down for a moment or two:

"If you are just a skeleton, you are still yourself, but nobody could tell by looking at you, because your looks are gone."

Here's a logical idea:

"Bones are what keep us from being too sloppy and relaxed."

A young man of a more scientific turn of mind made a discovery of his own about the heart:

"It is thought by most that there is but one heart for each of us. But I am thinking we may soon find others. I myself have felt them in my rist and head for two more. Some day others may find these and other places."

What's a brain for?

"The brain is what tells every thing else to get busy and do around."

What about the eyes?

"My eyes look out in the light and see things for my brain, where very little light exists."

And the ears?

"Without ears I would not be able to hear all the sounds I hear like WHOOoooo. Gik Gak. Eeeeaaaooo. FLIBEFLABOS. flibeflabos. But sometimes I am happy I have ears."

The nerves?

"Nerves are what we need to get messages up to the brain. And they let you face anybody and be a man."

If you're one of those people who keep intending to go on a diet but never do it, here's something to think about:

"A calorie is the heat needed to raise the temperature of one gram of water one degree. So people count their calories because if they eat too many of them, they will boil over."

Let's investigate a few more little-known "facts" about anatomy:

Blood keeps going because the heart keeps pushing on it and never lets it rest. I have known some people like this.

At first we eat to grow. After that is done it is more to be soshable.

Located between the neck and the schoulder is the clavichord.

There are 64 bones in our arms and only 62 in our legs. The mistake is yet to be found.

We humans are both vertebrates and mammals. You see we are smart enough to know how to be both at the same time.

The difference between bones and skeletons are the same except we live ones have bones while the dead ones have skeletons.

A naked eye is so small it cannot be seen unmicroscoped.

Light enters our eye through our corona.

Without brains, people would not even know enough
not to blow them out.

My digestive system is long and hollow but squisched
together until I grow more room for it.

We have nerves so that they can carry electrick volts
around in our body so it can get used to it.
Then if we run into to many volts, it takes
more of them to kill us than if we had not had
nerves.

Our brains look like chewed up bubble gum.

Blood vessels are teeny boats that carry blood all
through us.

Without lungs the body would not get the fresh air
it needs to live, so the lungs are on our side.

When you are standing, the tibia is just north of the fibula.

(*How much does the human brain weigh?*)
It depends on whether its a mans or a womans and I thought you were going to ask about the stomach.

Genes are things you have whether you want them or not.

Standing on your legs too long gives you very close veins.

The well rounded person is made up of both brains and bronze.

We breathe through our nostrums.

(*Of what value is the human heart?*)
It is good to listen to and talk about if nothing happened on the news.

Red spots on you can come from germs, or bites, or maybe you have an energy.

I try not to confuse adenoids with asteroids, being different in one way or another.

Hearts are useful for valentines and causing people to marry.

Man is really faster than we might think. Nerve signals can travel to the brain at about 200 miles an hour!! Misfortunately, we have not yet thought out how to run that fast with our outsides.

Even in pre-history, men and monkeys have always had four fingers and a thumb in common. That is they don't have the very *same* fingers and thumb in common, but a set to each so we don't have to pass them around or exchange them or oh skip it.

Unhealthy bodys are the dead kind.

The alimentary canal connects Lake Erie and the Hudson River.

Going down our human neck we find the sacoughagus, telling us when to cough.

The lungs keep breatheing in good air and making it bad and breatheing it out. It is human nature to be wasteful like this.

Your colateral is what you have behind you.

Let us consider for a moment the word chestfallen. Here is another tricky one. It is not at all what you might think since men are also sometimes.

You will get flat feet if any arches fall down on you.

While man has pores, mold has spores. It is one way to tell us apart.

The chest cavity in the body is called the borax.

We should all be grateful to Pasteur for inventing rabies.

CHAPTER 12

After a Siege of Health

THERE WAS a time when a kid submitted to a Saturday night bath—if his mother could catch him—and that was his one and only sacrifice to the ideals of health and hygiene. But kids today are at the mercy of well-meaning teachers, doctors and nurses who study, poke, prod and vaccinate them at every turn. Health is the watchword of the schools, and our reluctant kids are much the better for this new emphasis on soap and towel. Kids used to need excuses to stay *out* of school; now they need written explanations of their sniffles so they can stay *in*.

What do the kids think of this relentless drive toward cleanliness? Here's what one young health enthusiast wrote:

"One important health rule is to take a bath every day. I thought about it all last week."

157

Another student was nothing less than brilliant in explaining the difference between health and hygiene:

"Health is just keeping well while hygiene is being clean about it."

The boys and girls that I enjoy talking to the most aren't always the straight-A paragons who can be depended on to echo back all the right answers. The ones who are the most fun conversationally are the ad-libbers of the schoolrooms, those dauntless characters with free-wheeling imaginations who never hesitate to try their luck at guessing when they don't know an answer. I prize a good, top-flight, experienced guesser because he's learning to think things out for himself. He's not content just to sit back and

wait for teacher to fill in all the blanks in his knowledge. Instead, he studies a problem, fits together
what facts he already knows, and takes a long,
soaring leap to a conclusion. Guessers are glori-
ous chance-takers . . . and they're at their funniest
when they come a cropper, as these did:

"Angina Pectoris was a famous heart doctoress."

"The Hippocratic oath is when one swears never
again to be Hippocratical."

"Scurry is a disease caused by too fast living."

"One hypodemic equals ten epidemics."

"An epicure is used to cure epidemics."

"High places will give you highdrophobia."

"Hives are caused from fooling around with bees."

Another weakness of mine is for punsters—the ones
who pun unintentionally, like these:

"Now we know how to pasturize our cows by
milking them in pastures."

"Infantigo is one of the diseases of infanthood."

"Rats carry the blue bonnet plague."

"Don't forget to not look in the sun as you travel or
you will get a migrate headache."

"Infectious Hepatitis is a lover ailment."

Here are some more medical tips and ideas:

It is important to stay and get plenty of rest after a
siege of health.

False doctrine was like when they took blood out of
　　sick people.

Only doctors know how to unbutton belly buttons.

You must take it easy if your heart attacks you.

When they picked the bicycle off me I was found to have many critical cuts and bruises, but the sprung ankle was propably my best injury.

Meat helps build strong bones and muscles while carrots prefer to build your eyes.

When it rains we should take care to protect our bodies and our selves from it.

Appendecitis is caused by unflamed appendixes.

All those hotter than 100 are of a bad temper.

Tho we don't know it all yet, mankind is learning much about good health. We know for example that in order to live forever we need only —— This is as far as we have learned so far.

Many of the wonder drugs of the 1940s were known as Suffer Drugs but they were necessary to get well.

For anyone who actually wants to get as clean as possible, he should make sure to work the soap into a lathe.

Although we use oxygen to breathe, we do so knowing that it can cause rust. It is another case of a mixed blessing.

Sure iodine is bitter. But if we don't eat enough, gourds will soon grow in our throwts.

In order to prevent rabies, a rabid dog should be inserted in the bloodstream.

Inside each ear we have a hammer, an anvil and a stirrup. So the ears have a good excuse to ache sometimes.

The black plaque began with an acking in the middle ages and soon spread all over Europe.

Each generation is living longer than the one before it. Proof of this is the many more grandparents we see alive today as compared with great-grandparents.

One of the most painful of the minor injuries is the home grown toenail.

The more %centage of alcohol in your blood the worst you are. But don'd worry because you canot get more than 100% cent.

A bruise is caused when you hit or blow your skin.

Drowners are usually pretty soon saved by artificial presperation.

I have been vacinated for smallpox. Or against small-pox whichever is the usual custom.

Some doctors on the moon claim they know a way to reduce many 250 pd persons to only 42 pds.

It is healthiest to inhale deeply before you expire.

The people who suffer most are the ones with dis-eases in remote areas.

To stay healthy every day, we need plenty of fresh exercise. And be sure to get your share of sleep and air.

It does your body no good to rool it down the stairs.

Stay on the left side if you walk down a street. Don't let them get you from behind.

A trip is fine if you need a good relaxative.

(*What is first aid?*)
First aid is your chance to get better before the
doctor gets you.

Not enough vitamins causes a lot of rackets.

When people get old they can't bear children.

When your combustion is bad, you feel loggy.

Gout is caused by rich food. We should remember to
eat poor food.

We should worry more about our drinking of water
or we will all get polluted.

Doctors must be very careful to inscribe drugs because fatal doses can often be harmful.

CHAPTER 13

Some Trees Just Stand Around

O<small>NE OF THE</small> funniest skits that I've ever seen featured comedian Sid Caesar as a German doctor who was an internationally known authority on health. When a reporter asked him why some trees live hundreds of years longer than man, Dr. Caesar drew himself up proudly and explained:

"Good posture!"

To me, that line was a stroke of comic genius; and yet that's exactly the kind of thought a child might have about the long lives of the stately Sequoias. Listen to these on trees:

"Some trees give us berries or cherries or plums. Others are content to just sit and add another ring."

"All trees are either evergreen or broadleaf. If you are a tree, you have to make up your mind."

"The sequoias are the biggest of all Indians. One was so big they had to cut a road through him."

"Have you ever wondered how a cottonwood tree can have both cotton and wood in it? I will tell you that so have I."

Sometimes a new bit of information is turned upside down in a child's mind, and comes out like this:

"One reason for our scarecity of timber is because much of our timber supply is used in the making of forests."

Or this one:

"Trees come in forests that some people can't see them for."

Let's turn over a few more leaves, and see what we find:

One blade of rye has about four million roots if, streatched end to end, would surprise many people.

If a person is up against a cactus he must touch it. But if he is up against a tough proposition he does not have to be thus touching.

When you cover your housetop with leaves and vines and such, you have yourself a hatched roof.

In the Fall it is called that to let the leaves know what to do.

Many plants have been named after animals such as fox gloves, tiger lilies, and dandy lions.

An early spring wild flower is the trillium. There are about that many then.

How anybody could mistake fur tree needles for fur I will never know.

Balsam needles are so soft and flat that they are really not good for anything except balsam needles.

One way we can tell white pines and red pines apart is one has more needles than the other. Remember this and you can never mistake them for each other.

One of the prettiest but saddest sighted trees is the weepy willow.

Pine trees give us Christmas and Turpentine.

I don't know why they call the dogwood that unless because of its bark.

As soon as a tree has enough water and air, it can have a sort of sugar made. The sun then takes over and does the work while the tree does the rest.

Tree trunks have the purpose of connecting the leaves and the roots.

When winter comes, trees store all their sap away in trunks that they keep for the occasion.

Orchids usually grow fast to other plants (not quickily, but gripily).

The cotton plant has very thin threads called fibbers. Just because, I guess.

The kind of grass I am thinking of is a dark green kind. It might be any kind of grass on the other

hand, so long as the other kind is not the kind
I am thinking of.

Fig leaves are smaller than they should be.

The drabest appearing lawn can soon be changed
with a short swig of verbita.

There are two plants in the Thallus family, Algae Thallus and Fungi Thallus (both of a common sex).

Fall comes when the leaves are no longer tight.

Many of our weeds need some form of birth control.

Violets are not always. They may be whites or yellows.

Seeds should be buried whether they are dead or not.

By the time they get full grown, most wild roses are bushed.

Cotton must constantly be on the alert against attacks by the bold weavel.

Actually the stinging needles is not officeally called that. The person that named it made a mistake and spelled it a stinging Nettle.

Always keep your moss on the north side of a tree and you won't get lost.

CHAPTER 14

Pies, Squares and Wrecktangles

As I was going to St. Ives
I met a man with seven wives,
Each wife had seven sacks,
Each sack had seven cats,
Each cat had seven kits;
Kits, cats, sacks, and wives,
How many were there going to St. Ives?

Learning arithmetic at school used to be a fixed routine of counting apples and oranges, slicing up pies, and occasionally working puzzles involving such characters as the man going to St. Ives or that remarkable farmer-and-a-half who could plow an acre-and-a-half in a day-and-a-half. Then came multiplication tables, with the best kids learning their twelves, and lessons in pushing a decimal point around. Some boys and girls struggled even higher into the mysteries of mathematics, learning how to hunt down algebra's elusive character known as X, and trying vainly in geometry class to square a circle.

Today's kids must learn the same basic skills, but they are growing up in a whole new age of computers. As one girl said, "Thanks to our computers, we can now solve complicated problems by twinkling an eye." If only it were that simple! The truth is that now that we're having machines figure all our most difficult problems for us, we're also finding out that we need far more trained mathematicians to tell those computers what to do.

So now the question arises, how are today's future computer experts doing in the classroom? Judging by their examination papers, they're just as bewildered as any generation before them:

"A hypotenoose is a humane device for hanging criminals from a 90 degree angle."

"If your triangles get four sides you have wreck-tangles."

"In area, a circle is a pie or square."

Here's a statement that came straight from the heart of its frustrated writer:

"Pythagoras advanced geometry to the point where it is no longer understandable."

A backhanded compliment to the Arabs came out like this:

"The Moslems invented the zero and showed us how to think of nothing."

How would you define a circle? Here's as good a way as any:

"A circle is a square with all the corners smoothed out."

There've been many mysteries about the pyramids

of Egypt, but one scholar thought he'd unearthed yet
another one:

"Men in charge of these pyramids checked every
slab to make sure they were plum. A secret that dies
with them was plum what."

Suppose we "plum" a few more mysteries of arithmetic:

Why I am taking algebra is because I hear that some
thoughts cannot be thought without thinking in
algebra. Although I have never had such
thoughts, I am expecting.

I have never seen a square root, but, then, also, I
never dig trees.

Of course there are no such figures as 6/5's. They
are only figures of speech.

So as not to get mixed up, I always try to say integers in arithmetic because some girls as well as arithmetic have figures. But no girl integers.

If we were to take 17 and 4/8hs. from 22 and 2/4hs. we would have exactly 5 approximately.

The circumference will tell you how fat the circle is.

Arith. is like doing numbers only the problems are worked in a harder way. It is mainly for showing off.

A million is bigger than the largest known whale.

Ten meters equal a diameter.

Statistics show that the majority of P.T.A. members are married.

I have found infinity to be easier to say than what it means.

The minuend is the number from which the minuet is subtracted.

Axioms and postulates are the same. We have both
of them in case we forget the word for one of
them.

Triangles are often called isosceles to make them
sound more important.

When a period is surrounded by numbers it is a
decimal.

Because of numbers we can figure out what happens
if we have ten apples and do something. This is
important to some people.

When you multiply widths by lengths you don't have either any more. You have areas.

Square objects are rectangular while round ones are tubercular.

(*Since today is April 19th, what will the date be sixteen days from now?*)
It will be over to May the somethingth.

When we speak of a thing being mean, we know it is just the average of the way things are today.

When rulers are not human, they have twelve inched feet.

I am hopping for the day when we can have numbers without arithmetic.

A centipede is a worm measureable only in the metric
    system.

A square is where one of its sides is all the same.

A tangerine is a line going past a circle.

If you are looking for an X, algebra will help find it.

A circle should look good and round and come out
    even where it started.

Foot-pounds are how many you weigh if you are just standing on one foot.

(*When it is ten at night in Los Angeles, what time is it in New York?*)
I don't know. My mother makes me go to bed before then.

CHAPTER 15

Webster's Whoppers

O<small>N THE DAY</small> a child first learns to say "Mama," his own personal adventure into the world of language is well under way. He is already an expert in communicating in babyish ways, such as crying, fussing, laughing and gurgling. But now he is beginning to realize that there are different meanings for each word cooed over his crib, and that the sweet nothings murmured by his mother aren't really nothings after all. So from this day forward, a child reaches out with all he has to grasp every syllable that he hears. There will be hundreds of comical times ahead when he will stumble over meanings by mistaking one "sound-alike" word for another. Foreigners do the same thing. But teachers tell me that half-learning a word incorrectly is often the first step to learning it right . . . so let's be philosophical about riffling through the

following pages of Webster's Whoppers, and enjoy
this dictionary of fractured English:

A

ABSTAIN means to stop. But make them say what.
Those who are AMBIGUOUS can use either hand.
An ANCESTOR is an extinct relative.
ANOMALOUS has an abnormal meaning. We were
  never told what it was.
An AQUEDUCK is the kind that knows how to
  swim.

B

A BAMBOO is a thing useful to scare small kids.
BANDANAS are for bandats faces.
A BEDROLL is a pastry outdoorsmen like to take to
  bed with them.
If you are BILINGUAL you must only speak twiest
  a day.
The BRIGADIER GENERAL is the general in
  charge of the brig.
BUGLES are used by the Army to revile the troops.
BURDEN is where burs go for the winter.
A BUTTRESS is a lady butler.

C

Although I have heard of CHAPS that were people if they were English, they were worn around the legs if they were cowboys.

CLAIRBOYANT is playing like you can see things that aren't there.

COLLECTIVE . . . a plate they hand around at Sunday School.

A CORPORAL is the lowest noncommitted officer.

COTTON GIN is some hard coke made from the cotton plant.

A COURTSHIP is the royal boat where the king
   does it.

CURATE is how fast you get well.

A CURRENT is a seedless raisin found in electric
   wires.

D

DEPORT is to export without their wanting to go.

DISENGAGE is not to get married.

DUMB people, as we know, cannot talk. Some of the
   dumb ones I know can, yes, but they are the ex-
   ceptions that prove the rule.

E

ECLAIRS are cookies with insides.

ENTOMOLOGY is the study of how to entomb people scientifically.

EXCOMMUNICATION is done with paper bulls.

An EXPOSITION is the last job you lost.

F

FABRICATED is something that doesn't really exist
   like a fabricated house.

A FREUD is someone that claims he is somebody he isn't.

G

GAME PRESERVES are something like jello that you can play with if you want to before puting it on the toast.

GERMINATE is to visit Germany.

A GIGOT is a gigolo of the opposing sex.

A GOBLET is a baby turkey.

A GRAM is the weight of one of that type cracker.

H

HALF SISTERS are caused by magicians.

An HOBBY is something a person enjoys doing that is none of his business.

A HUMANE is a nicer type human.

There is no such thing as a HUMBUG but it is old and groachy when there is.

HYPOTHESIS is the name of an ancient guessing game. The Greeks played it all the time.

I

INCONGRUOUS means being elected to the Senate or the House.

INCONSISTANT means like tHiS.

An INTERNE is something like a backward U-turne.

IONS are certain kinds of electric particles. When they get old they change to eons.

J

A JAGUAR is a mammal. You can tell by feeling it's hair if you really want to know that bad.

The chief value of the JAPANESE BEETLE is yet to be discovered.

K

There is this word beginning with K that I remember the definition but I forget the word.

A KINESCOPE is a magic glass to look at your relatives and other kin through.

L

LATIN is the Language of the Dead.

LAUNCH is the one between breakfast and supper.
A LIVERY is a horse's skin made into a uniform.
A LOCKET is a lockable locker.

M

A MAGNATE is a big businessman who has such enjoyments as spinning a compass and pointing to the north pole.

A MALLET is a wooden-headed duck.

MAROON is a color that often gets lost.

A MIRACLE is something that can't happen until it does.

A MIRAGE is an optional illusion.

MOCCASINS are snakes that the Indians make shoes from.

MONKEY RENCHES are where they grow tame monkeys.

N

When a man makes up his mind to do a good thing and really does it, that is a NEW YEARS REVOLUTION.

A NICHE is what in time saves nine.

O

OGLES and OGRES are two horrible type monsters. But one just looks at you and the other one eats you.

An OHM is an English home.

OMNIVEROUS means jumpy like saying omniverous as a cat.

OUTLAWS are black-sheep inlaws.

P

PARTIAL POST is when they forgot some of the
mail.

A PERTINACIOUS is a thing that makes you believe
things. Woodrow Wilson had one of these.

PHARMACY is the study of pharming.

When a person has a PHOTOGRAPHIC MEMORY

it means he is able to remember anything he hears after only one time. It doesn't have to be repeated because it is not necessary to repeat it if he has a photographic memory.

PICKLES are a bit too much.

A PLASTIC SURGEON can take years off people by lifting their faces behind their ears.

A POTION is a portion of some southern type drink.

Q

QUARTZ is a very useful glassy-like mineral. Much of our milk is bottled in quartz.

R

Remembering a past experience is known as RE-COIL.

REINS are used mostly on horses. Only kings can use them on people and then only if they spell them reigns.

RESERVATION is a word spoken by Indians. What it means is "do you have a place to stay in this hotel?"

A REVAMP is a lady monster repaired to attract men again.

REVERE means to daydream. But not the Paul kind of Revere.

RIFF RAFTS are the kind that come apart in the middle of the water.

S

A SABLE is an expensive place to keep horses, being fur-lined and everything.

SCALES are found on snakes and pianos.

A SPINSTER is an unmarried wife.

A STAFF is a rod with a crook on the end. The crook has to stay either there or in jail.

A STEREOPTICON is a surgeon who prefers to operate by lantern light.

T

TAXIDERMOLOGY is the study of how to stuff taxis (with people, supposably).

TEAR can either be that you are crying or ripping. At least these and maybe more that I will tell you about when you tell them to us.

THANKSGIVING is for thinking about good things and being thankful for them even if you happen to be without any.

U

UNANIMOUS means not to be animous.

URANUS is a planet we find located somewhere near the universe.

V

VETERINARIANS are animals who were in the war.

VITAMINS are a way we can measure for no one getting malnutritious.

W

A WATERSPOUT is a wet tornado.

A WELL TEMPERED ax means that say there is a cherry tree. If it is well tempered it will not chop it down without good reason.

A WHALE is much larger than I believe.

X

X's are becoming close to extinct, being used mainly just for signing and kissing.

XERIC means arid when I can think what that means.

Y

While the YAK is taken for granted by many Tibetans, most authorities take them for mammals.

Z

In the ZEBRA we see how nature so wonderfully protects through protective coloration. It is presently threatened with extinction.

CHAPTER *16*

History on the Rocks

To most kids in grammar school, a fossil is anybody over the age of 35. The idea of even older fossils, the rocky kind that were formed millions and millions of years ago, just can't be grasped by boys and girls who are newcomers to earth themselves. Of course, man himself has learned to read the history of the earth from its geology only in the past century or two. Only now can we decipher from rocks the ancient dramas of great mountain ranges and even whole continents thrusting up above the seas, or plunging beneath the waves . . . of seas and islands that are no more . . . of great ice ages, and days when the northern regions had a tropical climate . . . of the timid, tiny creatures that first crept out of the oceans and became the ancestors of all the animals on land . . . and of the enormous dinosaurs that once walked the earth.

Geology is quite a complex subject, so it's hardly surprising that our school kids would become confused about it. Even adults are seldom sure about the difference, for example, between stalactites and stalagmites, so you can sympathize with the boy who dodged the question completely, like this:

"Hanging down and pointing up in some caves, we find satellites and satellmites."

One of the most intriguing things to me about a child's mind is not what he thinks but why he thinks it. Suppose a child learns in Sunday School that there is a devil in a hot place down below. Then on Monday the boy trudges off to school where he's told that the lava from volcanoes comes from a very hot place down below, inside the earth. It's only natural for him to put these two thoughts together and say what one boy said on his examination paper:

"Granite is made in a deep fire under the earth. I think you can guess who makes it."

Here's another bit of reasoning that seems to make sense:

"We call a small rock 'pebble,' and we call a big rock 'bolder.' Being bigger, they are."

And here's something I never knew before:

"Many rocks are made by the underground."

Did you know there are live caves as well as dead caves? Neither did I, but one boy assures us:

"You can tell if a cave is alive or dead by checking around its spelunks."

Here are more thoughts by junior geologists:

Caves are hollowed out by ground water, if the water
is ground just right.

Living things of our own time have not yet had time
to turn to fossils. Men in geology are waiting
anxiously so they can study them also.

A rock weighs less under water in case I ever want
   to know.

Some rocks have bands in them. The streaky kind.
No music.

It is against the rules to pick up a Petrified Forest.

To understand how lava works, I think of a cold lump of clay. I am not sure about it yet but I am still thinking.

All volcanos one day get old and die. After it has just sat there for awhile, all the heat goes. We call the rock around it igneous and that is that.

A great deal of our present-day supply of oil comes from underground.

Many of the dead animals of the past changed to dirt or oil while others decided to be fossils.

(*What might we expect to find at the bottom of a lake?*)
Stuff.

If all the salt in the ocean was piled together, there would be too much of it.

What lodestones are loded with are magnets.

Limestone is useful for building. Building buildings mostly.

Rocks made under water are called sentimentary rocks.

Mesomorphic rock is a long and skinny kind.

Batholites allow the formation of copper or

Most of our caves were made by water eating away
at the rock. Some of our larger caves show just
how much rock water can sometimes eat.

No living fossils have been found as yet.

With the discovery of fire, man learned how to make
rocks. These fire made rocks are called ingene-
ous rocks.

The most outstanding thing about sandstone is to
remember it can even be made under water.

Water can wear away a rock until it is completely unvisible. But dont expect it to happen in one class period.

Several crystals can sometimes be melted and hardened into one piece except they would no longer be crystals so you might just as well not.

Geysers are like us all and have to let off steam sometimes.

Quicksand is either waterey sand or sandey water, but it is to dangerus to really see which.

Basalt does not, as you might think, taste as you might think it might.

I know all rocks are very old. I do not know what they were as children.

A shamrock, of course, is not really one at all.

When a volcano erupts, what it erupts mostly is larva.

CHAPTER *17*

Chemists Anonymous

T<small>AKE ONE LITTLE BOY</small>, mix him up thoroughly with several pounds of strange facts, then shake him up with an examination, and you have the perfect formula for instant confusion. Whether you personally happened to sail through or sleep through your own classes in chemistry and physics, you'll probably find as much fun as I did in the next few pages of the better bloopers in the basic sciences. You'll find ideas and theories that have never occurred to the most eminent of modern researchers. You'll also discover, I suspect, that even such complex, no-nonsense subjects as chemistry and physics can become absurdly funny when seen through the eyes of children.

One blasé little fellow wasn't too impressed with what he was learning about the elements, so he wrote:

212

"After chemists went to all the trouble to learn how to mix iron and oxygen, they only came up with rust. So it doesn't pay to get too fancy."

Here's something else to think about:

"Some people use salt to freeze ice cream while others use it to melt snow. One day we will see who is right."

A warning came from a youngster who obviously thinks we are letting our scientific discoveries run away with us, for he said this:

"We must be careful about making too much nylon out of our coal, air and water. For what good would all the nylon in the world do us if we used up all our coal or air or water?"

Another budding young scientist was more optimistic, assuring his teacher that:

"I haven't worked out how to change salt water to fresh water, but I will do it this weekend."

Kids often ponder over puzzlers that adults would never think about, like this one:

"Some oxygen molecules help fires to burn while others choose to help make water, so sometimes it is brother against brother."

Here's a wild guesser at work:

"Photosynthesis is a way plants have of taking pictures of synthesises. Then they eat them."

There may not be a Nobel Prize winner in the lot, but I think the kids who wrote the rest of these deserve some kind of a prize for imaginative confusions:

In looking at a drop of water under a microscope, we find that there are twice as many H's as O's.

Another word for fire is oxidation, but I think I will just stick with the first word and learn it good.

Some unscruplus men have made aspirin and other medicines out of old coal tar!

There is nothing to keep a liquid from changing to another state. The Mississippi River, as we all know, does not have to stay in that state alone.

To most people solutions mean finding the answer, but to chemistists solutions are things that are all mixed up.

As water rains down on us, some either evaporates directly or is absorbed by vegetation and then evaporated from the plants. I know all of this and understand a little of it.

The chemicals in your body are exactly the same as those in the sea. This is something I won't know until I go to college.

A drinking tumbler can be made of glass or many other materials provided he is not the human kind of tumbler.

Here is something. If water is mixed with vapor it is lighter than air.

Water is the most common of everything we see.

The common table variety of vinegar is a weak solu-
tion of asthetic acid.

Coke is made by roasting soft coal in special ovens.
Pepsis are made something like this.

We must all learn to live together. The air has done
it. And paper and milk and soil.

Coal is made from sand and dead plants. Or if you
will wait some millions of years you will have a
diamond.

Bread gets mouldy because there is a whole glass of water in every loaf.

Atoms were first made during world war two.

One way to tell for sure if a sweater is of wool is to hold it over a flame. If it burnt slowly it was wool.

A molecule is comprised mostly of things.

As a puddle dries up, the water goes into the air. We
say that the puddle evacuates.

(*What condition exists when there is 100% humidity
in the atmosphere?*)
Everybody drownds.

With all the uses to be made of rubber it was necessary to find a substitute. After all, rubber does
not grow on trees.

CHAPTER *18*

The Savage Brest and All That

O NE OF MY favorite stories is about a concert violinist who went on a safari in Africa. After being separated from his party, he decided he might as well relax until they found him, so he took out his violin, sat down in the center of a large clearing, and began to play. Soon the animals of the jungle, entranced by the music, began stealing softly up through the bushes to form a circle around him. All their instinctive fears and hatreds were forgotten . . . a lion sat beside a wildebeest, a tiger next to a zebra, a monkey beside a leopard. As all the creatures sat there, great and small, spellbound by the music, a huge black panther suddenly leaped out into the center of the circle with a savage roar, seized the hapless

220

violinist and killed him. Whereupon the lion, with tears in his eyes, turned sadly to the panther and said: "How could you do a thing like this when that music was so very beautiful?" And the old panther said, "Hey?"

I was reminded of the unlucky violinist when I read this comment by a young music student:

"The violin is an instrument that is much too popular today."

Here are explicit instructions on how to play a rhythm instrument:

"It is easy to teach anyone to play the maracas. Simply grip the neck firmly and shake him in rhythm."

Another music student conjured up this vivid picture:

"Probly the first of all instruments were the percussive. Even in the oldest civilizations available today where we find nothing else, we find natives beating on their tumtums."

Speaking of "tumtums," one boy tells us this:

"Just about any animal skin can be stretched over a frame to make a pleasant sound once the animal is removed."

You'll hear many a new sound as we now continue our musical tour of the classrooms:

The baton (played by the conductor) is the most important of all instruments.

The lowest-noted strung instrument is the bass vile.

A sextet is oh you know.

It has been said that among all the instruments, the fife has one of the longest chronicles. Why this is so remarkable is how this could be in such a short instrument.

The harp has to vibrate to all the strings it has because of the shape it is in.

A cello is sometimes called a violincello by those who aren't sure which.

The english horn is neither english or a horn. Rather, it is an english horn because all the other instrument names had been taken.

Music is good because of the influence it has on the savage brest and all that.

Dirges were music written to be played at dirgeable launchings and crashes.

I understand about ray and me and fa and all the rest except dough. How do we know where dough is to start? Once I get started I know where to go, but it is in dough that I get mixed up.

To get the sound, accordions have bellows but they don't sound at all like that.

The spinet was an olden piano you could play or so on.

A bassoon looks like nothing I have ever heard.

Bataan is noted for its manufacture of musical conducting sticks.

I practise my piano every day unless it is rainy or sunshinny.

The virginal was a keyboarded instrument only certain ladies were allowed to use.

A oboe is a instrument popular with the poorer folks.

Friendshipwise, Mozart and Haydn were veryclose.

My favorite composer is Pablo de Sarasate. I am looking forward to hearing some of his music.

I would like for you to teach me to play the cello. Would tomorrow or Friday be best?

Most good singers have at least a two-octane range.

A thrombosis is an instrument you can make low sounds on a slide with.

(*Define syncopation.*)
Syncopation is not just boom boom. It is boom pa da boom or sometimes boom ca pa doodle da rest boom boom.

As if it was not enough to compose all the music he did, Schubert did it all within the short 31 years that he lived.

Podiums are somethings for conductors to step on. It helps their meanness.

A piece of music is always spelled piece. Peace and music never go together.

Minor keys are those allowable for children-composers under twenty-one.

It is not known for certainty who wrote the Third Symphony. Some say Brahams and some say Baithoven and some say let them both.

Since sound travels better through solid material than through water or air, music instruments are best when made out of solid materials rather than water or air.

Schubert didn't make much money and we would hardly have heard of him if he hadn't written some music.

My favorite instrument is the alto sex.

When I have nothing else to do, I like to go off by myself with Beethoven's fifth.

CHAPTER 19

Illiterature

Mark Twain once defined a "classic" as "a book which people praise and don't read." It's a funny line, but the joke is on Twain, because no less a writer than Ernest Hemingway once wrote that all modern American literature comes from one book by Mark Twain called *Huckleberry Finn*. So Twain stands contradicted by his own popularity . . . by the millions of boys and girls who love his classic work. As one boy wrote, "Huckleberry Fin was misfortunately borned into poor poverty. He is my favorite book so far."

Charles Dickens wrote so vividly that his characters came alive and stepped right off the page, which of course is the test of the finest characterization. This makes for exciting and rewarding reading, but youngsters are sometimes upset to find the "bad" people as real as the "good" people. Here's what one boy had to say about the characters in Dickens' *A Christmas Carol:*

"A real spooky story was to be found in this one about a man named Scrooge who has a night mare with goasts and chanes and everything. Others in the book are Tiny Tim and his father and mother and others. My crit. for this story would be it would be better if they left Scrooge out. It was because of him that things got bad and mizary pervailed. I might add that I saw the movie of this book last year, having liked it some better even after still using Scrooge."

Another youngster who learned that fiction was just that—fiction—had this comment:

"We now know that such people as Tom Sawyour,

Peter Rabbit and Robinson Cruiso never really lived at all. Many authors have made a good living out of fooling everyone."

Suppose we read a few more book reports:

Peter the goatherd asked Heidi to marry him. If you want to know what happened then, you must read "Heidi's Children."

Uncle Tom's Cabin is a good book for Simon Legree until the very last few pages.

Robinson Crusoe met Black Friday in 1929.

He knew she was likely to get into trouble and he wanted to help her.

The Big X was a fine book, but I don't want to tell you any more or it will spoil it for you.

The author then tells of going to visit his best friend in Boston, unknowing that he had been murdered decently.

This book that I finally finished over the week end was awful. The writer takes always and longer to say nothing and it's not very important after all that. I have the opinion that no writer should waste his time, much less others by making use of unnecessary words he doesn't need to get his message across.

A plagiarist is a writer of plays.

This is about the book I read. I don't remember it's exact name of the book but it tells about this boy that falls in love with this girl but then doesn't know what to do next.

I have always wondered if Robin Hood and Riding Hood were relationed.

By titling his poem "Leaves of Grass" Walt Whitman let us know it is poetry that is coming. If the title says something impossible we can know it is poetry and get ready for it.

When I read a poem now, I can usually tell whether the poet has iambic, trochaic or antipestic feet.

Poetry always comes out the same at the end.

Five accents to the line is antiseptic poetry.

One of Homer's best read poems is The Oddity.

The Iliad is a doctor's book about sick people.

I believe it was Little Ada who was a characteress in
Uncle Tom's Cabin. Since she was in fiction, she
really did not exist. While I am thinking of it
now, she possibly was not even the one in Uncle Tom's Cabin which would make her even
more of a fictional characteress.

Jason was a very rich man with golden fleas.

Kenilworth griped me intently.

(*What was the real name of Mark Twain?*)
O. Henry.

I am not sure who wrote The Devil's Disciple, but
this afternoon I will be where I can find out.

I think the greatest need in books today is one to
briefly review all of man's knowledge up to now
so we can get on with learning new things.

Romeo loved Juliet. Her balcony was famous.

Early in his War and Peace, Tolstoy proved he had
a very long drawn out tail.

All stories have morals if we will just look for them
hard enough. As a child, Goldilocks even taught
me. She taught me not to eat other peoples food
or get in other peoples beds.

THE END